THE TRAIL
WEST

Twocan

PICTURE THAT!

THE TRAIL WEST

EXPLORING HISTORY THROUGH ART

ELLEN GALFORD

Two-Can Publishing
An imprint of Creative Publishing international, Inc.
18705 Lake Drive East
Chanhassen, MN 55317
1-800-328-3895
www.two-canpublishing.com

Created by
Toucan Books Ltd.
3rd Floor
89 Charterhouse Street
London EC1M 6HR

Project Manager: Ellen Dupont
Art Director: Bradbury and Williams
Editor: Kate Simkins
Designer: Bob Burroughs
Proofreader: Marion Dent
Indexer: Sue Bosanko
Picture Researcher: Christine Vincent
Author: Ellen Galford
Series Consultant: David Wilkins

Library of Congress Cataloging-in-Publication Data

Galford, Ellen.
The trail West : exploring history through art / Ellen Galford.
p. cm. — (Picture that!)
Includes index.
ISBN 1-58728-442-1
1. West (U.S.)—History—Juvenile literature. 2. West (U.S.)—In art—
Juvenile literature. I. Title. II. Series.
F591.G214 2004
978—dc22   2004008334

1 2 3 4 5 6 09 08 07 06 05 04

Printed in China

CONTENTS

HEADING WEST 6

FRONTIER LIFE 20

TAMING THE LAND 44

HEADING WEST

IN THE EARLY 1840S, THOUSANDS OF SETTLERS FROM THE EASTERN UNITED STATES SET OUT FOR A NEW LIFE IN THE WEST. THE LONG AND DANGEROUS ROUTE WILL TAKE THEM THROUGH PRAIRIES, DESERTS, AND HIGH MOUNTAINS.

PICTURE THIS: THE YEAR IS 1845. You live on a farm just outside a small town in the eastern United States. You were born here. Your grandparents, aunts, uncles, and cousins live close by. This is the only place you know. You have never traveled more than a few miles from home.

Everyone in your family works very hard, including you. Before and after school, you have many chores to do. Still, there is never quite enough money to buy the things your family needs. Your parents think life would be better if they had a bigger farm, but there is no land nearby for them to rent or buy. Then, one day, your father says that it's time to head west.

Since the early 1600s, Europeans have come to America and settled along the East Coast. Slowly these people have spread westward, clearing the woodlands and starting new farms. In 1803, the United States bought a large area of grassland that stretched west from the Mississippi River toward the Rocky Mountains. This area is called the Louisiana Territory. Beyond Louisiana, the wilderness continues all the way to the Pacific Ocean. Some of this land is owned by Mexico. Other areas have been claimed by Great Britain, France, or the United States—and sometimes more than one country.

Apart from a few fur traders, the first Americans to get to know the West well were

THE WAGON TRAINS that begin rolling west in the 1840s change the face of the United States forever. Places once considered too wild or too far away are now within reach. The people who make the trip are changed forever by this daring adventure.

MERIWETHER LEWIS AND WILLIAM CLARK explored the land west of the Mississippi River. They returned with tales of a rich, fertile region with plenty of good land for anyone who wants to start a farm.

Meriwether Lewis and William Clark. Between 1804 and 1806, these explorers traveled all over, studying the land and making maps. The United States government then encourages people to follow in the explorers' footsteps.

With the help of Lewis' and Clark's maps, families make their way west, choose a piece of land, and set up homes and farms. Native Americans have lived on these lands for thousands of years, but most settlers believe the land is free for the taking.

Your parents think this chance is too good to miss. So that spring, your family packs your belongings and some supplies into two covered wagons. You join a long line of wagons heading west on a 2,000-mile (3,200-km) route called the Oregon Trail. It stretches from Independence, Missouri, all the way to the Oregon Territory, on the West Coast.

There are no roads to travel on, and sometimes not even a track to follow. But the people leading the wagon train know the way.

To lighten the load on the wagons, you and your family walk most of the way.

The trip takes many months. You camp out each night beneath the stars. You see strange and wonderful sights: huge herds of buffalo, soaring mountains, and plains that seem to go on forever.

DURING THE WINTER of 1804–1805, Lewis and Clark spent many months living with the Mandan people, including Chief Mató-Tópe. The Mandan people lived on the plains in the area that is now North Dakota.

THE WAGON TRAIN

THE TRIP WEST IS A DANGEROUS JOURNEY INTO the unknown. Those who make the trip are called emigrants, a name for people who leave their home to settle in a different country. The West seems like a whole new world to those living in the East.

Pioneer families, like those shown in this painting by Benjamin Franklin Reinhart, find safety in numbers. They form long lines called wagon trains, or convoys. A wagon train is led by a guide who knows the territory well. One of the largest wagon trains leaves Missouri in the spring of 1843. Known as the Great Migration, a train of more than 100 wagons, 1,000 adults and children, and 5,000 cattle sets out for the Oregon Territory. It will take them nearly six months to travel 1,800 miles (3,000 km). They have to cross swift rivers, wide prairies, and high mountains. A few forts along the route offer the only chance to stock up on fresh supplies, rest the animals, and repair battered wagons.

This painting was made in 1867, but it shows an earlier time, probably the 1840s. Everyone in the convoy seems to know exactly what to do to prepare for nightfall. They are moving the wagons into a protective circle, feeding and watering the animals, and preparing their own supper before darkness closes in.

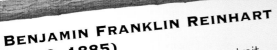

BENJAMIN FRANKLIN REINHART (1829–1885)

Benjamin Franklin Reinhart became a portrait painter at the age of 19. He lived in New York City but made many trips to the West. He painted landscapes and scenes of everyday life like the one shown here. He also produced portraits of famous people, including the Native American princess Pocahontas, of the Powhaten nation.

THE EMIGRANT TRAIN BEDDING DOWN FOR THE NIGHT, 1867
BENJAMIN FRANKLIN REINHART

WHAT'S COOKING? This woman is using her kettle to heat water for washing. Soon she will need to use it to cook supper. The pioneers have brought foods that should not spoil during the long, hot trek: flour, beans, beef jerky (dried beef), dried fruits and vegetables, and slabs of bacon. People bury their chickens' eggs in barrels full of oats to protect them from cracking on the rough journey.

WATER OF LIFE Wagon trains try to stay close to rivers so that they always have fresh water. (Rivers also help keep them from getting lost.) Emigrants on their way to California have to cross the desert, so they plan their routes based on the location of springs, where fresh water flows out of the ground.

BEASTS OF BURDEN Oxen and cattle provide most of the muscle-power to pull the heavy wagons across rough ground. Depending on the weight of the load, it may take between six and twelve pairs of oxen to pull one wagon. (Mules and horses are also used.) Wagons normally travel at a human's walking speed, although a good wagon driver can sometimes make the animals go faster. With rest stops, a convoy expects to cover 12 to 15 miles (20 to 25 km) per day.

READY TO ROLL The large wagons are long and narrow and are topped with canvas. They appear to "float" through waves of tall prairie grasses like a sailing ship, which earns them the nickname "prairie schooner." The covered wagons are crammed with tools, food, clothing, and a few prized possessions. When the going gets rough, families lighten the load by throwing out anything that they don't need to survive. Abandoned furniture becomes a familiar sight along the trails.

THE GRASS IS GREENER This man has harvested prairie grass to feed the convoy's livestock. By 1845, the grasslands are not able to keep up with the needs of the wagon trains. Guides agree to limit the size of wagon trains and stagger their leaving dates, to make sure there is enough grass available.

MOTHERHOOD Children often outnumber adults on a wagon train. In nineteenth-century America, large families are common. In one Illinois prairie community, nine out of ten mothers report having at least five children. Three of those ten women have ten or more young mouths to feed.

FUR TRAPPERS

FROM THE LATE 1700s ON, THE UPPER MISSOURI RIVER VALLEY attracts people with a spirit of adventure. Explorers such as Lewis and Clark (see page 7) were among the first Americans to see the area that will become the states of Wisconsin, Michigan, and Minnesota. These men tell stories of forests and riverbanks teeming with animals that are prized for their skins or fur. Such stories lure other men to head west to seek their fortune. Some become trappers, hunting beavers and other animals. Traders buy the pelts from trappers and sell them for a profit. Fur hats and coats were prized by people in Europe.

This painting shows two fur traders returning home from an expedition. The man paddling the canoe comes from a French settlement north of the United States. He is married to a Native American woman, and the boy is their son. Most traders and trappers learn survival skills such as hunting and navigating from the natives they meet in their travels. It is not uncommon for these men to marry Native American women.

FUR TRADERS DESCENDING THE MISSOURI, 1845 GEORGE CALEB BINGHAM

MYSTERIOUS **MASCOT** Almost everyone who has seen this painting has puzzled over the little animal on a chain. The animal appears to be a cat, but if you look very closely, you can see it has a bear-like face. Whatever it is, the animal's mother was likely killed for her fur, and the traders decided to keep the young animal as a pet.

MEAT ON THE MENU The boy has shot a wild duck, which will make a tasty meal for him and his father. Fur trappers and traders survive on whatever plants and animals they can find. The trunk that the boy is leaning on contains the furs they have collected upriver. The skins of beavers, bears, foxes, deer, muskrats, otters, mink, and wild cats are in great demand around the world.

SMOKE SIGNALS The man is holding a clay pipe between his lips. Whether or not he likes tobacco, he uses smoking as a tool to help him find his way through the wilderness. With no maps to guide them, trappers and traders measure distances by the time it takes to smoke a pipe. "Our camp," they might say, "lies two pipes downstream from here."

GEORGE CALEB BINGHAM (1811–1879)
George Caleb Bingham grew up on the frontier in Missouri. He began his career as a portrait painter, specializing in painting the important citizens of Washington, D.C., Philadelphia, and other eastern cities. His greatest success as an artist came when he began to capture the daily lives of the people he had grown up with— farmers, fur traders, and boatmen on the river.

HUNTING BISON

IN THE WEST, MILLIONS OF AMERICAN BISON, OR BUFFALO, ROAM THE PRAIRIES. Native Americans depend on this shaggy animal. They eat its meat and drink its milk. Its hide, or skin, is used to make clothes and blankets, the tents they live in, even the lightweight boats they use to fish the rivers. Other parts of the animal are made into ropes and bowstrings. People carve its bones into weapons, tools, and ornaments. The bison is also an important part of native religious beliefs.

The hunters in George Catlin's painting are hiding under wolf skins as they prepare for a surprise attack. They will silently thank the bison at the moment their arrows bring the animals down.

The white settlers and their rifles are a serious threat to the bison's survival—and to the way of life of the natives of the plains. Hunters kill the animals by the hundreds for their valuable hides. By the 1830s, there are no bison east of the Mississippi River. By 1880, herds in the West are nearly wiped out as well.

BUFFALO HUNT UNDER THE WOLFSKIN MASK, 1832–1833 GEORGE CATLIN

GEORGE CATLIN (1796–1872)

Pennsylvanian artist George Catlin spent five years traveling through the West, painting the faces, costumes, daily lives, and religious rituals of many different native tribes. When he had an exhibition of his artwork in London, England, he combined it with a Wild West show that featured Native American performers.

COMPETITION Bison survive on the wild grasses of the plains. As more and more wagon trains start to make their way west, the settlers' livestock compete for food. Along the trails, the land is soon stripped bare. Bison herds shrink as many of their grazing grounds disappear.

POWERFUL CREATURES OF THE PLAINS A male bison can weigh more than 2,200 pounds (1,000 kg) and reach a shoulder height of 50 feet (1.5 m). Ancestors of the bison first came to North America from Asia sometime between 800,000 and 200,000 years ago. At that time, a land bridge connected the two continents. Bison once roamed throughout North America.

IN DISGUISE The Native Americans of the plains greatly admire the hunting skills of the wolf. They believe that if they wrap themselves in wolf skins when they hunt bison and other animals, they take on the powers of the wolf.

TROUBLE ON THE TRAIL

T HIS PAINTING, LIKE MANY OTHERS PRODUCED IN THE MID-1800s, satisfies the public's desire for tales of bloodshed and drama in the dangerous Wild West. It also helps spread the false belief that all encounters between pioneers and Native Americans are violent.

Many clashes do occur between the natives and the newcomers, whose wagons and livestock push across tribal lands in ever-growing numbers. But that is only part of the story. Many encounters between the two groups are friendly.

In the early 1840s, when the first groups of pioneers traveled westward across the Great Plains, the natives and the travelers were curious about each other. Many Native Americans offered the strangers advice about the safest routes, good places to find water, and plants that were useful as medicine or food. Sometimes they traded goods.

The relationship between the natives and the pioneers begins to change after 1849. That year, the discovery of gold in California lures tens of thousands of settlers onto the trail. Native Americans watch in horror as the prairies, the wildlife, and their own lives are changed forever. No longer do they feel so friendly toward these strangers.

CHARLES FERDINAND WIMAR (1828–1862)

Charles Ferdinand Wimar was born in Germany, but his family moved to Missouri when he was a child. As a young man in 1851, he returned to his homeland, where he painted pictures of clashes between Native Americans and pioneers. He did not actually visit the West until he returned to the United States in 1856.

THE ATTACK ON AN IMMIGRANT TRAIN, 1856
CHARLES FERDINAND WIMAR

A FAMILY AFFAIR The people tending to this woman are likely her own relatives. Many wagon trains are made up of family groups. Often several married couples—brothers and sisters with their wives, husbands, and children—team up to head west together.

A VIOLENT END When Native Americans and pioneers did clash, the natives were more often killed by settlers than the other way around. Although records are likely incomplete, documents from 1840 to 1860 list 362 pioneers and 426 Native Americans who died in such conflicts.

S HIELDED FROM DANGER These Native Americans are carrying shields made from buffalo hide. To make them, they use the thick skin from the animal's neck. For extra protection, they paint their shields with symbols such as bird claws that are believed to have special powers.

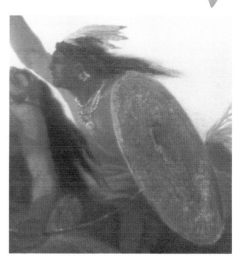

SAFETY IN NUMBERS In this imaginary battle scene, Native Americans are threatening a convoy of several wagons. In real life, large and well-organized wagon trains are rarely targets for violence. When attacks do take place, they are usually aimed at much smaller groups, such as a hunting party that has wandered too far from the trail.

HIRED HELP The man aiming the pistol is dressed differently from others in the group. His fringed deerskin suit suggests that he may not be a newcomer to the trail, but rather an experienced frontiersman hired as a guide. After 1849, thousands of single men head west to search for gold. Like this man, many of them join family groups. They earn their keep by driving wagons or tending animals.

A TOOL FOR WAR AND PEACE The Native Americans' small axes, called tomahawks, are used not only as weapons but also as tools for everyday tasks, such as chopping wood. The word *tomahawk* comes from the Algonquin people, who lived in the eastern United States before the Europeans arrived. Early tomahawks have stone heads tied to wooden shafts. The tomahawk shown here has an iron head, which would have been brought to North America from Europe by traders.

FRONTIER LIFE

SETTLERS WORK HARD TO MAKE THEMSELVES AT HOME ON THE FRONTIER. BUT EVEN THESE WIDE OPEN SPACES HAVE TO BE SHARED WITH NEIGHBORS—BOTH OTHER NEWCOMERS AND NATIVE AMERICANS.

PICTURE THIS: THE YEAR IS 1850. YOU LIVE WITH YOUR FAMILY in a one-room log cabin that you have helped to build. A large fireplace is all you have to keep you warm. Every drop of water for drinking, washing, and cooking has to be carried in a bucket from a stream nearby.

This new home is much more comfortable than the one you lived in when you arrived on the frontier. For the first few months, the whole family crowded into a temporary shelter that was little more than a shack. Clearing land for a farm, plowing up the hard soil, and planting seeds is more important than building a nice house. Your parents have to make sure there will be enough food

EVERY FRONTIER farmer's wife keeps chickens. Eggs and the birds themselves supply fresh food, while the feathers are used to stuff pillows.

for the family and the animals on your farm. Once that is done, your father chops down trees and splits the wood into logs for building a cabin. Everyone but the babies is expected to help.

Your first winter here is hard. You don't always have much to eat. If someone in your family gets sick or hurt, there is little anyone can do. There are no doctors for hundreds of miles. Families do their best, and neighbors help each other when they can. Still, many people on the frontier die without proper medical care.

As time goes on, life on the frontier gets easier. The crops on the farm have grown well, and your family has more to eat. Sometimes there is

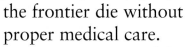

THE CHEYENNE are friendly to the settlers until large numbers of Europeans begin to take their land. The tribe begins a bitter war with the settlers that ends only when the Cheyenne surrender in 1877.

even enough time to play. You begin to think of this place as home, even though your life is very different than the one back east.

Life changes for the Native Americans who live here, too. In the early days, many welcome the newcomers. They teach them about the plants and animals living on the land. The explorers Meriwether Lewis and William Clark (see page 7), for example, had help from a Shoshone woman named Sacajawea. She guided them across the plains and helped them communicate with many native groups.

Natives such as the Mandan live peacefully with their new neighbors. They are happy to trade animal furs for metal tools and other useful things. But as thousands of Europeans come flooding across from the eastern United States to settle in the West, Native Americans begin to feel frightened. They realize that many settlers do not want to share the land but to take it all for themselves. The natives realize that their own way of life is in danger. As a result, it becomes harder for settlers and natives to be friendly. Sometimes (although not as often as people think), angry natives defend their land by attacking the wagon trains.

WHEN SETTLERS build a new house or barn, neighbors come from far and wide to help, then have a party when the work is done.

THESE CARVED WOODEN figures represent a pioneer man and woman. Unlike women living in the eastern United States or in towns at that time, this pioneer wife wears a short skirt. She also knows how to shoot a gun.

A Cabin in the Wilderness

LIKE SO MANY FRONTIER FAMILIES, the French-Canadian settlers in this painting by Cornelius Krieghoff have cleared a patch of land and built a home out of logs. The typical pioneer cabin does not follow the style of Native American lodges and long houses. It looks more like a home found in northern Europe. In the region that is now the state of Delaware, seventeenth-century emigrants from Sweden built log houses very much like the ones in their homeland. Other settlers copy this style, and log cabins soon pop up in forested areas all across the United States and Canada.

Log cabins are well suited to pioneer life. Wood is easy to find and free for the cutting. The cabins are quick to build and simple to put together. Neighbors often help each other.

The first task is to peel the bark off the logs. Bark holds moisture, and if it is left on the wood, the house will feel damp. Next, simple notches are cut in the ends of each log. Once this is done, the logs can be stacked on top of one another. The notches hold the logs together at the corners of the building. Any gaps and open spaces between the logs are filled with clay or a thick paste of clay and wood chips.

Cornelius Krieghoff (1815–1872)

Painter Cornelius Krieghoff emigrated from Holland to New York in 1836 and worked as an artist for the U.S. War Department. After marrying a French-Canadian in 1840, he settled in his wife's homeland. He specialized in painting landscapes and scenes of the everyday lives of French-Canadian settlers.

SETTLER'S LOG HOUSE, 1856
CORNELIUS KRIEGHOFF

HEAT SUPPLY Every cabin has a lean-to or a woodshed to keep logs dry. The kind of wood used as firewood depends on what trees grow nearby. Pine is the easiest to light. A fire made from a harder wood, such as oak or elm, takes longer to get going. However, these logs burn more slowly than pine, so the fire lasts longer.

CUT TO SIZE A section of a split log lies on the wooden sawhorse, ready to be cut into lengths short enough to fit the fireplace indoors. The tool for this job is a bucksaw, seen here leaning against the sawhorse. The bucksaw has two wooden handles, one long and one short. Some large saws need two people to handle them, but this one is designed for one person.

AN OPEN AND SHUT CASE The wooden shutter on this window will be closed at night for warmth and safety. The family who lives here is lucky to have panes of glass in their window, especially with so much snow outside. Other cabins have only square openings for windows. For those families, shutters are the only protection against rain, snow, and wind.

FUEL DELIVERY The ox rests after pulling home a sled piled with fresh timber. The sled's ropes are slung over the animal's horns and fastened to a small headpiece fitted on its forehead. Surprisingly, travel is often easiest in winter. An ox can pull a sled across the snow much faster than it can pull a cart along muddy tracks in spring or autumn.

SLIPPERY SLOPE These two children are playing with a tiny sled that was probably made for them by their father. It is very similar in shape to the large one the family uses to carry logs. At this time, all sleds are homemade, but few are as well crafted as this one. Many are nothing more than flat pieces of wood or an old tin tray from the kitchen.

RAFTS FOR THE FEET The farmer has just taken off his snowshoes, which help him move across the snow without sinking in. People in areas with snowy winters began wearing snowshoes about 12,000 years ago. Early Native Americans made them from pine branches. Later versions, like these, look more like tennis rackets, with tightly woven strands of animal gut stretched across a wooden frame.

AT HOME BY THE FIRE

T HIS PEACEFUL SCENE OF HOME LIFE SHOWS A FUTURE PRESIDENT OF THE UNITED STATES, ABRAHAM LINCOLN, AS A TEENAGER. It was painted by Eastman Johnson in 1868, three years after Lincoln died. This fireside scene would have looked familiar to almost anyone who grew up in rural areas of the United States during the first half of the 1800s.

In a log cabin, the large kitchen fireplace is the heart of the home. It usually occupies one whole end wall of the building and is topped by a huge chimney to draw up the smoke.

Without this glowing fire, life on the prairie—or any place where nights and winters are cold—would be impossible. The day when electricity or gas will provide the energy for people's homes is still far in the future. So, like other frontier families, the Lincolns would have relied on those log-fed flames to keep them warm, cook their food, and provide light for reading.

EASTMAN JOHNSON (1824–1906)

Eastman Johnson was born in Massachusetts. He had little formal training but taught himself the art of portrait painting. He worked mainly in charcoal, crayon, and chalk. In his twenties, he traveled to Europe, where he was inspired by great Dutch painters such as Rembrandt.

FOOD FOR THOUGHT The book that young Abraham Lincoln is reading probably did not belong to him. Books are hard to come by, so people often pass them from family to family. Its original owner may have bought it from a book agent who travels and sells books door to door. In the early 19th century, around 90 percent of the books bought in the United States are purchased this way. By the 1830s, it is possible to buy some books by mail order. The first public libraries in the United States are not built until 1852.

PRESSING MATTERS The small, heavy flatiron being heated near the fire will be used to press the wrinkles out of freshly washed clothes. Women usually need two or more irons to deal with a single load of washing. One is left to heat while the other is in use. Mrs. Lincoln's spare flatiron sits on the high shelf above the fireplace. In many homes, Monday is wash day, and Tuesday is spent ironing.

BOYHOOD OF LINCOLN, 1868 EASTMAN JOHNSON

A MANDAN VILLAGE

IN THE 1830S, THE ARTIST GEORGE CATLIN TRAVELS ALL OVER THE WEST, meeting many different native tribes. He makes friends with chiefs and warriors, paints their portraits, and learns about their lives. When he comes to the village in this painting, on the upper Missouri River in what is now North Dakota, he is fascinated by what he finds.

Unlike other Native Americans on the plains, the Mandans do not move their camps to follow the bison herds. Although they hunt bison, they are also farmers, growing crops such as maize and tobacco. They live in large settlements surrounded by wooden walls. Their villages serve as local centers for trade with other native groups nearby. The Mandans are friendly with many settlers and traders.

Unlike other plains Indians, the Mandans live in houses built of timber and earth. They also dress in beautiful clothes, make pottery, play a variety of ball games, and enjoy home comforts such as steam baths.

They even spend time relaxing, often on the roofs of their houses. George Catlin climbed up to the top of one of these buildings with his sketchbook to capture this beautiful view of the settlement.

GEORGE CATLIN (1796–1872)

George Catlin wanted to record everything he could about the Native Americans on the Great Plains. He knew that their way of life was being threatened by the wave of white settlers moving into their tribal lands. Catlin created what he called his Indian Gallery—a collection of 500 pictures painted to preserve details of a world that he feared would soon be lost forever.

BIRD'S-EYE VIEW OF THE MANDAN VILLAGE
1,800 MILES ABOVE ST. LOUIS, 1837–1839
GEORGE CATLIN

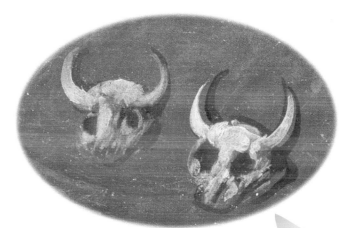

DOUBLE PROTECTION As a shield against evil, two bison skulls are placed on top of the medicine lodge, a building used for religious ceremonies. They are also placed on some of the houses. In order to release their power, there has to be one male and one female skull in every pair.

GREAT EXPECTATIONS If this child misbehaves, he will probably be praised instead of punished. Mandan parents want their sons to be strong-willed and independent. They believe that a boy who gets into fights or talks back to his elders is likely to become a mighty warrior.

STRONG MEDICINE The poles rising high above the village are called medicine poles. They are decorated with war trophies and other prized objects, including eagle feathers, weapons, dyed cloth, and the scalps of enemies removed in battle.

PILLARS OF THE COMMUNITY
Whenever a new house is needed, the women of the village take charge of the project, planning the work and giving orders to the men. The wooden timbers supporting the earth lodges are so heavy that it takes up to 20 men to haul one into place. Once the building is completed, it is expected to last for seven to ten years.

GIFT OF A LIFETIME
These two men standing on the roof are dressed in robes made from bison hides. Those worn by chiefs and warriors are decorated with colored beads, locks of human hair, and painted scenes showing their bravest deeds and other great moments in their lives. One Mandan leader gave George Catlin one of these treasured robes as a mark of friendship.

HOME IN A DOME
The Mandans' round houses, known as earth lodges, are made of a framework of cottonwood posts covered with branches, dried prairie grass, and a thick layer of soil. Each lodge is 40 to 60 feet (12 to 18 m) in diameter. Inside, sleeping rooms line the walls, separated by curtains. Smoke from the fireplace in the middle of the room is drawn out of the lodge through a hole directly overhead. In good weather, people use their rooftops for extra living space.

A Sacred Festival

O N A DEERSKIN, A KIOWA ARTIST NAMED SILVER HORN painted images of the festival known as the Sun Dance. For most Native Americans on the plains, this is the most important religious event of the year.

The Sun Dance takes place in late spring or early summer, and members of different native groups come from far and wide. It is a chance for old friends to meet and for different communities to come together in peace. Details of the Sun Dance vary from tribe to tribe, but the purpose and meaning of the festival is the same for everyone. It is a time of prayer, sacrifice, and thanksgiving.

The setting for the Sun Dance is a large circle, often enclosed by a wall of branches. In the middle of this space stands the medicine pole, a forked tree trunk hung with sacred objects such as an eagle's nest or a bison's skull. For those taking part in the ceremony, the pole acts as a bridge between earth and heaven.

For three or four days and nights, the men dance without stopping to eat or drink. They dance to earn good fortune and power, not only for themselves but also for their people, for the animals they hunt, and for the earth itself. All the while, they try to keep their eyes focused on the medicine pole.

SILVER HORN (HAUNGOOAH) (1860–1940)

Silver Horn, son of a Kiowa chief, was born in southwestern Oklahoma. At the age of ten, he began to paint detailed pictures of many different aspects of Native American life. By the time of his death, he had produced a series of more than one thousand images.

THE CAMP CIRCLE—MEASURING THE POLE , c. 1900
SILVER HORN (HAUNGOOAH)

BRANCHING OUT Only a pile of leafy branches marks the place where the tree chosen as the medicine pole once grew. Depending on the group that is holding the Sun Dance and where they live, the tree might be cottonwood, willow, aspen, or cherry. Whatever the wood, the trunk has to form a perfect fork.

A SACRIFICE This man has killed a bison, and its remains can be seen in the upper right-hand corner of the painting (see page 33). After saying a prayer of thanks to the animal, he has cut off strips of its hide to bring back to the camp. These are used to make a bison-shaped sculpture that will be displayed proudly on the pole.

MASTER OF CEREMONIES After cutting the tree, the medicine man leads a ceremonial procession. He wears a robe made from a bison hide and carries a fan decorated with eagle feathers. Both bison and eagles are held in great respect. They are considered guardians of the tribe and sources of supernatural power.

SOCIAL CIRCLE A circle of brightly decorated tepees surrounds the medicine pole. These tents are for the leaders of the different native groups who have come together for the Sun Dance. The only tent that has not been painted in vivid designs is the white one on the left. This belongs to the medicine man, who will lead the ceremonies.

MAKING THE CUT A procession approaches the tree that has been chosen as the medicine pole. Next to the tree stands a small figure carrying the hatchet. She is a captive woman from another tribe, and it is her job to chop down the tree. At the moment the hatchet touches the tree, the medicine man, who is shown standing just behind the woman, will recite special prayers.

JUST FOR FUN

FRONTIER FARMERS WORK HARD AND HAVE LITTLE FREE TIME. When they do have some time off, their idea of fun is to compete against their neighbors to see who is the fastest, the strongest, or the best at something. They run races to prove how fast they can move. They wrestle to test their strength. They challenge each other to log-splitting contests and see who will be first to turn a pile of tree trunks into a neat stack of wooden fence rails. One of their favorite pastimes is a shooting contest, like the one shown in this painting of Missouri life by George Caleb Bingham.

Bingham shows the players getting ready to take their turn aiming and firing at a target. The prize for the best shot will be to have the first choice of the meat when the cow in the picture is killed.

The man with a sharpest eye and a steadiest hand will bring home a valuable prize for his family. The winner usually chooses the "fifth quarter," which includes the animal's hide and the fat, known as tallow. He can sell the hide for a profit to a trader or a local tanner (a craftsman who specializes in turning animal skins into leather). He will probably bring the tallow home for his wife or daughters to melt down and make into candles or soap.

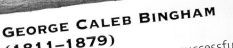

GEORGE CALEB BINGHAM (1811–1879)
George Caleb Bingham was a successful painter whose work hung on the walls in many wealthy western homes. He also was a politician. He was elected treasurer of the state of Missouri in 1862. His many pictures of Missouri life include all sorts of subjects, from political campaigns to farmers and fur traders.

SHOOTING FOR THE BEEF, 1850
GEORGE CALEB BINGHAM

PRIZE BEEF Fresh beef is a rare treat. Many farmers own only one ox, which is used to pull the plow. Their cow is kept for milk. If they want red meat for dinner, they have to go hunting for deer. Otherwise, they may kill one of their chickens or catch fish in a local stream for their dinner.

KEEPING THINGS HANDY This leather pouch is known throughout the West as a possibles bag. It provides convenient storage for small objects—anything from chewing tobacco to a snack for lunch. A powder horn, which keeps gunpowder safe and dry, fits into a slot in the top of the bag. The whole thing is worn slung around the neck from a leather strap.

SHARPSHOOTERS Men who are good shots take pride in their rifles. They give them names, such as Black Snake, Hairsplitter, or Panther Cooler. The men taking part in these contests rely on their shooting skills to win. But they also claim that certain weapons are better or luckier than others. Neighbors bet small amounts of money on the guns they think are most likely to win.

FOREST CLEARINGS The soil in woodland areas is fertile and easy to plow. To clear new ground, farmers chop down the smaller trees and hack away bushes and saplings. For larger trees, settlers use a method learned from the Native Americans. They cut a deep gash all the way around the trunk, which eventually kills the tree. Then they plant their crops around the remaining roots and stump.

FOUR-LEGGED FARMHANDS Like the human members of any farming family, the dogs of the West have to work hard to earn their keep. They guard the property, help to herd livestock, and go hunting with their masters. They might be well-loved companions, but they are more than just pets.

SCHOOL DAYS

A SCHOOL LIKE THE ONE IN WINSLOW HOMER'S PAINTING is a sign that a frontier settlement has turned into a real community. People have to work together to make sure there is money to build the school, make repairs, and pay the teacher.

Some teachers live in rooms attached to the school where they work. In many rural areas, families take turns in having the teacher as a guest in their house, providing meals and a place to sleep.

For students, the typical school lesson consists of repeating aloud whatever the teacher teaches them until they have learned it by heart. Older children listen to younger ones repeat their lessons while the teacher is busy elsewhere.

Discipline at school is strict. Children sit on hard benches and are rarely allowed to move around the room. Teachers punish naughty or lazy children by hitting them with a stick.

Yet even the harshest teacher has to let the children go out at lunchtime. The boys in this painting are enjoying their freedom by playing a game of Snap the Whip. Players hold hands in a long line. Then the leader drags the others along, making wild, quick turns until the children at the end fall down.

SNAP THE WHIP, 1872 WINSLOW HOMER

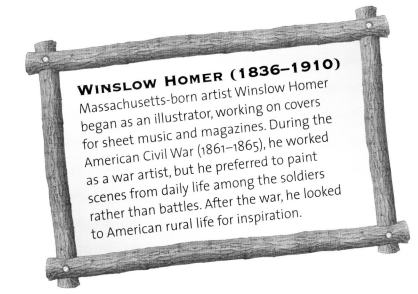

WINSLOW HOMER (1836–1910)

Massachusetts-born artist Winslow Homer began as an illustrator, working on covers for sheet music and magazines. During the American Civil War (1861–1865), he worked as a war artist, but he preferred to paint scenes from daily life among the soldiers rather than battles. After the war, he looked to American rural life for inspiration.

ALWAYS IN FASHION The boys' clothes— long-sleeved shirts, trousers with suspenders, and caps—look exactly like those worn by their fathers. By the time young people reach school age, they dress in exactly the same style as their elders. Most of the clothing worn here is probably handmade by the boys' mothers. Their hats were either ordered through the mail or bought from a store in the nearest town.

BAREFOOT BOYS Most of the boys in the picture are barefoot. Throughout the 1800s, shoeless children are a familiar sight in cities and countrysides alike. Families with little money try to make footwear last as long as possible. One way to keep shoes from wearing out is to use them only for special occasions and for going to church on Sundays.

THE LITTLE RED SCHOOLHOUSE

One-room schoolhouses are found in all rural areas of the United States. Students range in age from 5 to 18 or even 20 years. Older children whose farm work has made them miss a lot of school will come back year after year, determined to finish their education. Sometimes the teacher is younger than the oldest members of the class.

PLAYTHINGS For most rural children, toys are a special treat. The few toys they own are inexpensive or homemade items, such as this girl's wooden hoop. She rolls the hoop along the ground with a stick. Most games the children play, such as tag or hide-and-seek, involve lots of running around. These boys have fallen off the end of the "whip" in a lively game of Snap the Whip.

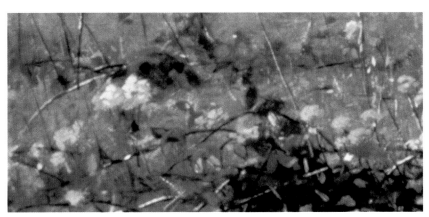

ABSENT FRIENDS? The carpet of grass and flowers underfoot suggests this scene is taking place in spring or summer. The time of year when everything is green is also the busy season for farmers. Many families keep their boys at home from spring until early autumn, because they need their help with farm chores.

TAMING THE LAND

TO SETTLERS, THE FRONTIER IS A LAND FULL OF PROMISE. SOME PEOPLE HOPE TO PROSPER BY PLANTING FIELDS AND BUILDING NEW COMMUNITIES. OTHERS DREAM OF GROWING RICH BY FINDING GOLD.

PICTURE THIS: YOUR FAMILY HAS SETTLED ON A FARM in the western United States. When you first arrived, everyone worked hard to make a clearing in the woods and build a small, temporary house. Within two years, the plot of land is hard to recognize. It has turned into a busy farm, with many animals and fields full of grain. Similar farms have sprung up nearby.

Since you left your home in the East, there has been no school for you to go to. Now, all the parents in the area get together and build a one-room schoolhouse. It is three miles (5 km) from your home, and the only way you can get there is to walk—rain or shine. Near the school there is a new church and a blacksmith shop, where iron tools and horseshoes are made. Best of all, there is a general store. The store sells everything you can think of, from coils of rope and peppermints to ladies' hats. It is a special treat for many families to make the long trip into town to shop and visit friends.

Throughout the western territories, everything is changing. In 1848, gold was discovered in California. Fortune-seekers from all over the United States and even other countries are rushing west to join in the hunt for gold. They buy up whatever land is available.

The United States government wants settlers everywhere to succeed. It does everything it can to make Native Americans give up their hunting grounds. Some of them give up their land quietly, while others rage fierce battles. By the end of the nineteenth century, most Native Americans have been moved onto reservations. These are areas of land in the West that the United States government has set aside for them. Often, these reservations have

ON MAY 10, 1869, at Promontory Point, Utah, the tracks coming westward from Nebraska meet the tracks coming eastward from California. At a special ceremony, the two sets of tracks are joined together with a spike made of solid gold.

AFTER GOLD WAS DISCOVERED IN 1848, people head to California from all over the world, hoping to strike it rich. They search for gold in streams, using flat pans and special tools. These Chinese workers came to the United States to build the railroads but stayed on to join the hunt.

poor soil and little wildlife, and it is hard for people to find enough food. Some are forced to leave their families and take low-paying jobs on farms or ranches. Native Americans everywhere struggle to hold on to their traditions, skills, and beliefs.

But the greatest change you see comes with the growth of the railroad. Ever since the 1840s, when the first passenger trains begin to run on tracks back east, people dream of the day when trains will rumble across America. Workers come from as far away as Ireland and China to do the heavy, dangerous work. They drag iron rails across rough ground, swing heavy hammers, and blast tunnels out of rock.

The trip that took your family six months will soon take just a few days. You wonder if people born in the twentieth or twenty-first centuries will ever be able to picture what it was like before this land was tamed.

AS MORE AND MORE people settle in the west, small towns sprout up to supply their needs. Farmers and their families come to shop, attend church, and meet up with their neighbors.

AT THE TRADING POST

I N 1837, THE ARTIST ALFRED JACOB MILLER TAKES A TRIP through the western wilderness. When he reaches the trading post at Fort Laramie, in the territory that is now part of the state of Wyoming, he finds that he has arrived at a very exciting time.

The gates of the fort are wide open, and the huge inner courtyard is crowded with people. He sees Native Americans of many different tribes, French-speaking fur traders, hunters and trappers from up and down the East Coast, and settlers seeking land farther west.

Laramie is one of several forts that has been set up by fur traders as a base for doing business with Native Americans. In the 1840s, these forts begin to serve a new purpose: a stopping place for wagon trains. There, emigrants can rest, repair their wagons, and stock up on fresh food and supplies.

Miller arrives during one of the three or four big trading weeks that are held at Fort Laramie every year. At these times, Native Americans and white traders come together to exchange goods. So Miller takes out his sketchbook and records everything he sees.

ALFRED JACOB MILLER (1810–1874)

American artist Alfred Jacob Miller made a breakthrough in his career when he joined an expedition to the western wilderness. The 166 detailed sketches he made on this journey provided the basis for the paintings of western subjects that he would produce throughout the rest of his working life.

INTERIOR OF FORT LARAMIE, 1858–1860
ALFRED JACOB MILLER

FRIENDS REUNITED For the Native Americans seated around the fire, a meeting at the fort is as much a social event as it is a time for trading. They enjoy the chance to exchange news, display their crafts, tell stories, and visit with old friends. According to the artist, the first day of a trading week is nothing but a party. After the fun, everyone gets down to business.

SPECIAL DELIVERY The mule carries a pack full of goods for trading. Native Americans swap animal hides and furs for goods such as gunpowder, tobacco, and glass beads. These highly prized beads are known as "pony beads," because native traders bring them home on the backs of pack ponies or mules. Most of the beads come from factories in Italy. Native peoples work them into beautiful designs to decorate clothing and containers.

TAKING NO CHANCES Hidden inside the fort just below the guard tower is a pair of cannons. Nobody expects them to be used on this friendly occasion, but everyone knows that they are there. The small openings in the wooden tower are gunports. Each one is large enough to allow a man inside to aim and fire a weapon, but small enough to shield him from enemy fire.

PORTABLE POSSESSIONS

Because this is a peaceful meeting, this Native American, possibly from the Kiowa tribe, has set aside his spear. The long wooden pole, tipped with a sharp wedge of bone, stone, or metal, is used both for warfare and for hunting. Because their clothing is made without pockets, Native Americans carry whatever they need in a basket, a bag, or a pouch like the one hanging next to the spear. The man also has a powder horn. He will probably buy gunpowder to refill the powder horn while he is at the fort.

HIGH HOPES Things must have been
fairly calm at Fort Laramie at the time this picture was painted. In more troubled times, this rifle would not have been hanging so far out of reach. Most rifles used by traders, fur trappers, and settlers are made in the Eastern states of Pennsylvania and Virginia.

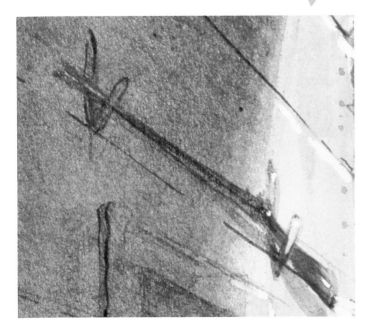

DRESSED FOR THE OCCASION The
Native American's leggings and cape are made from the skins of deer or antelope and are fringed with dyed porcupine quills or bird feathers. He has decorated his long hair with round objects known as *conchas*. These silver ornaments, originally worn by natives living farther south, are just coming into fashion among the plains nations at this time.

LIFE IN THE SADDLE

For those who travel the western trails, or raise animals on the prairies or in mountain pastures, the secret of survival is a good, fast horse.

In the 1800s, herds of wild horses roam the West. These animals are descended from horses brought to North America by Spanish explorers in the 1500s. Over the years, a few horses escaped to breed and flourish on the rich grass of the western prairies. Native Americans and cowboys like the one in this painting have learned how to capture, tame, and breed them.

These horses weigh between 600 and 1,300 pounds (300 to 600 kg). They are most prized for their tremendous speed. The horse shown here, urged on by a flick of his rider's whip, almost looks as if it is flying.

Cattle ranching is a growing business in the West. Leather and beef are both valuable to settlers on the frontier. And no rancher can work without a good horse. Together, a horse and rider must rope calves for branding, round up herds of cattle, and drive the herds to new grazing grounds or to market.

A single, skilled cowboy on horseback can handle 250 to 350 cattle at a time. But most cattle drives are made up of 2,000 or 3,000 animals, requiring 8 to 20 cowboys. A drive of this size can travel 10 to 15 miles (16 to 25 km) in a day.

COWBOY, c. 1890 FREDERIC REMINGTON

ROPING THEM IN The coil of rope hanging from the rider's saddle is called a lariat. The name comes from *la riata*, the Spanish word for rope. The man uses his lariat to catch animals. Roping is a skill that settlers learned from Mexican cowboys.

FREDERIC REMINGTON (1861–1909)

Frederic Remington was born in the eastern United States, but he is best known for his images of the Wild West. These vivid paintings and dramatic sculptures of horses, cowboys, Native Americans, and soldiers capture the energy and excitement of life on the frontier.

QUICK ON THE DRAW The cowboy keeps a handgun in a holster on his hip. He has to be ready to protect himself or his animals from rattlesnakes or other dangers. The holster is open at the bottom so it will fit a gun of any size. This hole also allows rainwater to run straight through, helping to keep the pouch and the gun dry.

SOLVING A THORNY PROBLEM The rider wears loose leg coverings called chaps over his pants. Chaps protect his legs against thorns, cactus spines, and bushes. Most cowboys wear chaps made of leather. But people who live and work in colder areas of the West, such as Montana, prefer warmer, shaggier versions like these, made from the skins of sheep or goats.

A HANDY WIPE The cloth the cowboy is wearing around his neck was often called a wipe. It would have been made of cotton, linen, or silk. It serves as a towel, a handkerchief, and a napkin. Keeping it around his neck rather than in a pocket makes it easy to pull up over his mouth and nose in a sudden dust storm, or to block the clouds of dirt kicked up by cattle.

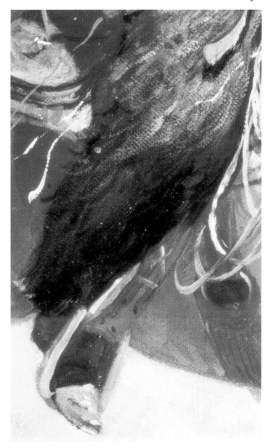

GOLD RUSH

O N JANUARY 24, 1848, A MAN NAMED JAMES MARSHALL takes a break from his work. He is overseeing the construction of a sawmill near Sacramento, California, in the Sierra Nevadas. He is also an amateur geologist, or rock scientist. As he walks along the American River, he spots some sparkly rock in the riverbank. After a closer look, he confirms that he has found gold.

As the news of the discovery spreads, treasure hunters from all over the United States head west. By 1849, what becomes known as the Gold Rush has begun. In that year alone, 80,000 would-be gold miners—also called the Forty-Niners—arrive in California. By 1853, there are 250,000 people in the state digging for gold in gravel beds and streams. A few of the miners, such as Charles Nahl, are also artists. This is one of his many paintings of miners at work.

Some settlers make their fortune from the miners instead of gold. They sell the hard-working goldseekers mining tools and clothes, and supply them with hot meals and clean laundry.

By 1864, the gold rush is over. Much of the gold in California has been removed. Only some large mines remain. Many of the camps set up by miners grow into permanent settlements. Other camps turn into "ghost towns"—rows of buildings left empty when the gold runs out.

CHARLES CHRISTIAN NAHL (1818–1878)

Charles Nahl came from a family of German artists, and he showed his early paintings in Paris, France. He arrived in California hoping to find gold. He never struck it rich, but his paintings are some of the most vivid pictures of life among the miners. For this painting, he worked with fellow artist Frederick August Wenderoth.

MINERS IN THE SIERRAS, 1851–1852
CHARLES CHRISTIAN NAHL AND
FREDERICK AUGUST WENDEROTH

L AND CLAIM The miners in the painting are working together on a "claim"—a piece of land that they have chosen for mining. Once this property is registered in their names with the government, nobody else is allowed to mine it.

H ARD WORK One of the miners is using a tool called a pickax to break up boulders into smaller pieces. This doesn't require special skills, but it is hard work, especially in the summer heat.

T HE CABIN Miners often share one-room cabins like the one shown here. They build these with their own hands, using wood from the forests nearby. Four or more people may eat, sleep, and store their possessions in a space measuring less than 16 by 20 feet (5 m by 6 m).

HOT AND THIRSTY WORK Mining is back-breaking work. This miner is taking a break for a much-needed drink of water. Miners wear hats in the summer months to protect them from the hot California sun. Their loose-fitting shirts and pants are made to be tough yet comfortable.

HIGH GROUND The mountainous landscape where the miners are working is part of the Sierra Nevada mountain range. These mountains divide California from what is now the state of Nevada. Here, jagged peaks tower over mighty rivers, beautiful valleys, and grassy meadows.

FINDING THEIR FORTUNE
The miners work in streams and gravel beds. In this picture, they are using a wooden box called a sluice. The sluice works like a sieve. The men shovel soil into the box. Water from the stream flows through it, washing away dirt and gravel. Since gold is very heavy, any nuggets of the valuable metal settle into ridges in the bottom of the sluice.

THE END OF THE LINE

MORE THAN ANYTHING ELSE, THE RAILROAD is responsible for taming the Wild West. In the eastern states, railways have been carrying passengers since the 1840s. In the 1850s, people called surveyors—experts in planning how land will be used—map out the first routes west.

The railroad companies have an enormous task ahead of them. Before any trains can run, workers must prepare the ground, blast tunnels out of rock, build bridges over rivers, and lay tracks. They must work long and hard in the wildest weather conditions and on the toughest landscapes. Their work has many risks, and some people lose their lives just doing their jobs.

Still, laborers come to the United States from all over the world to work on the railroad. Many of the workers come from China. They travel thousands of miles across the Pacific Ocean to escape starvation. They send most of their earnings home to their families in China.

Finally, in 1869, the two coasts are linked by rail. Settlement in the West will be easier than ever before. The country will feel more like one community. Only the Native Americans are not celebrating. They know this "metal road" will only mean more problems for them—and the buffalo on which they depend.

In 1899, the proud owners of the Denver and Rio Grande Railroad send a Missouri artist, Oscar Berninghaus, on a grand tour of their whole system. This painting of a small but busy western station is one of a series he creates to show the company's trains, the landscapes they pass through, and the places they serve. In this particular place, many methods of transportation are represented. A stagecoach, a covered wagon, and men on horseback have all turned up to meet the train.

WESTERN RAILROAD STATION, C. 1899
OSCAR EDWARD BERNINGHAUS

OSCAR EDWARD BERNINGHAUS (1874–1952)

Artist Oscar Berninghaus began his career sketching local scenes for newspapers in St. Louis, Missouri. During most of his life, he spent winters working as a commercial artist in St. Louis and summers in New Mexico painting landscapes and images of Native American life.

TAKING IT IN
STAGES A stagecoach
is waiting at the station to
carry passengers to their
final destinations. Before
the railroad, stagecoaches
were the main form of
public transportation in
the West. In out-of-the-way
places, stagecoaches
continue to run until 1910.

DELIVERING THE GOODS These crates and barrels probably contain the produce of local farms and ranches, ready to be transported to the eastern states. Trains are the fastest way to move farm goods from the West and to bring in factory products from the East. By the 1850s, railroad companies make most of their money carrying freight. There are six to ten times as many freight cars as passenger cars on every line.

ALL ABOARD For passengers like these, rail travel is much more comfortable than a slow and bumpy trip by covered wagon. Every passenger car on the train has its own stove for heat during winter months. Train travel is also much faster: about 18 miles (30 km) per hour rather than 12 miles (20 km) per day.

ON THE RIGHT TRACK Railroad tracks consist of two iron rails lying across flat lengths of wood known as sleepers. In good conditions, the workers lay between 2 and 5 miles (3 to 8 km) of track every day. But in the mountains, a day's progress was sometimes measured in inches. Some crews have worked on the same stretch of track since the trains started running, checking for problems and repairing or replacing broken rails.

A WAY OF LIFE UNDER THREAT
For the Native Americans in these tepees, the coming of the railroads is not good news. It is ruining their hunting grounds and encouraging more settlers to head west. In 1881, the company that owns the station in this painting—the Denver and Rio Grande Railroad—runs its lines across Native American territory but refuses to pay for taking their land.

FAIR WARNING
Many railroad lines run on unfenced routes through open country where livestock graze. After cattle cause several serious train crashes, an American mechanic invents the cowcatcher—an iron grill that can push an animal off the tracks. This kills the cow, but it keeps the train and its passengers safe.

GLOSSARY

convoy a group of vehicles, such as wagons, traveling to the same place together

emigrant a person who leaves their home to move to a new place or country

expedition a trip organized to explore an unknown place

fertile rich in nutrients and good for growing things

frontier an area that is just beginning to be settled. In the 1800s, the American frontier lay west of the Mississippi and Missouri rivers.

geologist a scientist who studies rocks

Great Plains a vast, grassy region in North America, east of the Rocky Mountains. It is also called the plains or prairie.

hide the thick skin of a mammal, such as a cow or a buffalo. The hide of these animals is often removed and made into leather.

immigrant a person who is making their home in a new place or country from where they were born

livestock animals raised for food or for farm work

long house a long, low wooden home built by some Native American nations in the eastern United States and Canada. Often it was large enough to house several families.

medicine man a Native American who serves as a religious leader and healer

mule a four-legged animal that is half-horse, half-donkey,

TIMELINE

1803 Louisiana Purchase—France sells the huge Louisiana Territory to the United States

1804–1806 Lewis and Clark explore the West

1832–1833 George Catlin paints *Buffalo Hunt under the Wolfskin Mask* (pp. 14–15)

1845 George Bingham paints *Fur Traders Descending the Missouri* (pp. 12–13)

1834 The Indian Territory is established in what is now Oklahoma. Thousands of Indians are forced to move.

1846–1847 Mexican War—The United States declares war against Mexico over valuable land in the South and West. The U.S. gains Texas, New Mexico, and California.

1850 George Bingham paints *Shooting for the Beef* (pp. 36–39)

1800

1812–1814 The War of 1812— The United States goes to war with Great Britain over ownership of land that is now part of Canada

1825

1837 John Deere invents the first steel plow. It is lighter and easier to use than an iron plow.

1837–1839 George Catlin paints *Bird's-Eye View of the Mandan Village* (pp. 28–31)

1847 Thousands of Mormons flee to Utah to avoid pressure from other religious groups

1851–1852 Charles Nahl and Frederick Wenderoth paint *Miners in the Sierras* (pp. 52–55)

1850

1856 Charles Wimar paints *The Attack on an Immigrant Train* (pp. 16–17)

1856 Cornelius Krieghoff paints *Settler's Log House* (pp. 22–25)

often used to pull carts or carry heavy loads in the West

nation a group of people, such as Native Americans, who share a certain way of life and often live together as a community

pasture an area of land covered with grass and other plants where animals such as sheep and cattle graze

pioneer the first person to do or try something new

prairie a wild, grassy, and mostly treeless area, especially that of central North America

procession a line of people marching or walking together

region an area of land or a specific part of a country

rural having to do with the countryside

sacrifice something of value that is given away, especially as a gift to a god in a religious ceremony

tepee a tall, cone-shaped tent made of animal skins that was used as a home by Native Americans living on the plains

territory an area of land claimed by one or more individuals or groups. The term was used in the nineteenth century to define areas of land claimed by the United States government but not officially organized into states.

wilderness a wild area with no houses, farms, or towns

1858–1860 Alfred Miller paints *Interior of Fort Laramie* (pp. 46–49)

1861–1865 U.S. Civil War

1862 President Lincoln signs the Homestead Act

1867 Benjamin Reinhart paints *The Emigrant Train Bedding Down for the Night* (pp. 8–11)

1868 Eastman Johnson paints *Boyhood of Lincoln* (pp. 26–27)

1872 Yellowstone National Park is established

1872 Winslow Homer paints *Snap the Whip* (pp. 40–43)

1875 Battle of Little Big Horn— General Custer leads an attack against the Sioux Indians. Custer and all 263 soldiers are killed.

1875

1876 Mark Twain writes *The Adventures of Tom Sawyer*, about a boy growing up in Hannibal, Missouri

1870 The Fifteenth Amendment gives all African-American men in the U.S. the right to vote. White women in the states of Wyoming and Utah also have voting rights.

1869 The transcontinental railroad is completed

c. 1890 Frederick Remington paints *Cowboy* (pp. 50–51)

1884 Susan B. Anthony urges Congress to give all women the right to vote

1890 Wounded Knee Massacre—U.S. troops kill as many as 300 unarmed Sioux travelers. This brings an end to decades of war between Native Americans and the U.S. military.

1883 The first skyscraper is built in Chicago, measuring 10 stories high

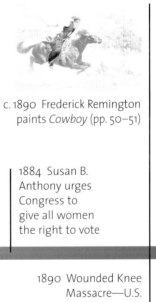

c. 1900 Silver Horn paints *The Camp Circle* (pp. 32–35)

1896 A discovery of gold in the Klondike River causes a new gold rush, this time in northwestern Canada

1900

c. 1899 Oscar Berninghaus paints *Western Railroad Station* (pp. 56–59)

FURTHER READING

Davis, Kenneth C. *Don't Know Much About the Pioneers.* New York: HarperCollins, 2003.

Duncan, Dayton. *The West: An Illustrated History for Children.* Boston: Little, Brown, 1996.

Haslam, Andrew. *Native Americans.* Make It Work series. Chanhassen, Minn.: Two-Can, 2001.

Hayden, Kate. *Plains Indians.* My World series. Chanhassen, Minn.: Two-Can, 2002.

Josephson, Judith Pinkerton. *Growing Up in Pioneer America.* Minneapolis: Lerner, 2003.

Lamar, Howard Roberts. *The New Encyclopedia of the American West.* New Haven, Conn.: Yale University Press, 1998.

Morley, Jacqueline. *How Would You Survive in the American West?* New York: Franklin Watts, 1996.

Murray, Stuart. *Wild West.* Eyewitness series. New York: Dorling Kindersley, 2001.

Paterek, Josephine. *Encyclopedia of American Indian Costume.* New York: W. W. Norton, 1996.

Rubel, David. *The United States in the 19th Century.* New York: Scholastic, 1996.

Sandler, Martin W. *Cowboys.* New York: HarperCollins, 1994.

WEBSITES

Pioneers and Life on the Frontier
www.oregon-trail.com
Great historical information on the Oregon Trail, pioneer diaries, and links to information on the Gold Rush

www.campsilos.org
Links and information on the native prairies and pioneer farming

www.pbs.org/weta/the west/
Materials and information to complement the PBS documentary, "The West"

http://library.thinkquest.org/6400/
Information on pioneer life written by students for students

www.eyewitnesstohistory.com

Artwork of the Period
www.corcoran.org
The Corcoran Gallery of Art, Washington, D.C.

www.metmuseum.org
The Metropolitan Museum of Art, New York

www.americanart.si.edu
The Smithsonian Museum of American Art, Washington, D.C.

Native American Resources
www.si.edu/resource/faq/nmai/start.htm
The Smithsonian Institution on Native American History and Culture

http://falcon.jmu.edu/~ramseyil/native.htm
Native American history and historical documents, and links to tribal sites